While
Dancing Feet
Shatter
The Earth

Keith Wilson

While
Dancing Feet
Shatter
The Earth

Published by
Utah State University Press
Logan, Utah

Library of Congress Cataloging in Publication Data

Wilson, Keith, 1927-
    While dancing feet shatter the earth.

    I. Title.
PS3573.I457W47   811'.5'4   77-13792
ISBN 0-87421-095-X
ISBN 0-87421-096-8 pbk.

ACKNOWLEDGEMENTS

Some of these poems were previously published in *Ahora, Arx, Cafe Solo, Camel's Hump, Colorado State Review, Desert Review, Evergreen Review, Expatriate's Review, From a Window, Granite, Grande Ronde Review, Frontiers, Hanging Loose, Human Voice, Intransit, Kayak, Monk's Pond, New Mexico Magazine, New Mexico Quarterly, New Mexico Review, Ninth Circle, Open Letter, Outsider, Poetry, Poetry Now, Potpourri, Prairie Schooner, Primer, Sumac, Star-Web Papers, Symptom, Tolar Creek Syndicate, Westways,* and *Wild Dog.*

—to my family

—to Frank Waters and my brother and sister New Mexicans

Contents

New Mexican Stones

The Gift

—for my daughter Kathleen

This is a song
about the gift of patience

of opening

the need to walk alone
ever, deeper, into

This is a poem
against light

a recommendation
to darkness

Bring a candle
the room is warm

This is a song

New Mexico: Paso por aqui

—Arthur Conan Doyle

Such might be said of this land
by those whose eyes fill to trees,
light buds caught in gentler winds.

These sweeps of sandstone, lava, cracked
mountains holding in themselves darkness,
great canyons

        buzzards flapping
against stiff winds, golden scorpions
high, clear skies
—old gods that look down
their turquoise eyes
glittering

This is an old land, dry & brittle.
Its charms are bones, hollowed to whistles,
dancing feet hidden by rising dust.

Here, we live uneasily, aware the sun
has stripped us, we know our bones
our dry flesh that whispers as we walk.

The skull of a cow
pared to a white clarity.
Snake, coiled in the rocks
his rattle another whisper, a reminder
that we are not alone, do not
alone own this land, nor walk
upon it too freely. It is held
the Indians used to say, by God.
All men are visitors here.

There is Bill, my friend,
his long legs dragging dust,
the way they dangle from the smooth sweat
of the mule's back

          there, is Bill and the
Canyon, the empty space both before him
and behind, him skidding along the slick trails:
the descent having its nature,
the fall from something, an entity.

*　*　*　*

The blue mouths of the thousand canyons
open for the fallen sun: an orange drop
it balances sweetly on the lips

          —is gone, leaving
thin light behind. There may be no coming
back from here: the mules, they carry flames
on their descending backs, the wool
of a mountain sheep is touched as he darts,
burry and bursting orange-black with grail
—as he leaps from jagged rockedge to glass
shining peak.

Rock eagles, uneasy winged bright birds,
beaks of mica, feathers of obsidian, watch
dying shadows hungrily

      who watch now

*　*　*　*

Tall and straight grow fossil palms, locked
in rock the giant lizards, hooked toes rooted
in granite . . . in the living rock of the great
Canyon's stride, eternities bind their blood
to stone.

        In the darkness stand unquiet
flowers. No god moves here. The blue-grey air
humming with threads of orange is a still construct,
potential as the fall of a poised boulder.

       *   *   *   *

Who has caught the sun?
Who has stopped the almost god
flashing through the millenniums
the eternities laid on in strata of rock?

Below, which stonebound, lumbering beast
now stirs, rose-red out of the shadows,
moves clumsily to shade and jolt these Canyon
walls with his heavy, earthen feet?

       *   *   *   *

Flames ride the backs of mules. Bill riding also
is a thin line, the mast of a burning ship. Clipped
shale clatters beneath the mule's hooves,
the just risen moon is a thin arc above the Canyon's edge:
a gesture, an old smile presents the gesture, and a good
-bye! for Bill, leaving all behind, who behind all left
something hanging in the air, turning, spinning the darkness
below into history, a quiet night riding at his back.

The Dark Gardens of Cuernavaca

In the sad Gardens of Cuernavaca
beside the pool with its hidden glow
Mad Carlotta tells her beads and he,
Maximiliano, paces the flagstoned path
dreaming of a Mexico cut from crystal.

The Aztec face of this land has not
changed, grows no older than age is.
The rivers go heavy with mud, desert
winds cut down the flowers that choked
the ruined palaces of emperors and kings.

Within the dark gardens of Cuernavaca
Chac Mool stalks his raingod heaven.
Blossoms like skulls hang heavy.
Mad Carlotta tells her beads, the tiny
Prince plays with a ball, tosses it,

pretending to a world imperial. Lost
these shadows tell no stories, walk through
halls blazing with decoration, bowing
heads, the aging trappings of dead royalty.
In the garden *Chac Mool* has eyes of stone.

The Only Photograph

I have before me your distant face,
on horseback, riding away, sixteen
years old with two blazefaced horses
and a well to mark old memories.

You're on this postcard that was meant
to be mailed to somewhere, someone,
not me, but I received it when you were
seventy-two and could no longer, my father,
sit a horse. Some gesture I did not
understand, nor properly look at
lies in the flex of that boy's hand
as he raises the horse's head up
and looks back through his blue eyes
to me
       most of his face shadowed by his hat,
the scratches the years brought you, my father,
are on the picture and frozen there.

Earl C. Wilson
July 4, 1970

The Voices of My Desert

Beginning this new trail, with the resonance
of shifting earth about me, I hear calls
distancing the crow voices of my childhood,

the wolf cry of my middle age. The sun
is an ancient symbol above me and God knows
what the mountains, spirit blue on the horizon

mean. Silence stands within me as without
desert stirs to its own subtle communication.
There is time, always, to wonder, doubt.

New Mexico is a myth, an ancient whirlpool
of time where moments stand still just before
being sucked down to other planes, other hours.

We hold time back through rituals, dances
that stir the seconds like flecks of sand
beneath our feet, eternities of the possible.

I write down the words I hear, but I know
it is the Dead who speak them. Our ears
are tuned to the past, hear, hear the days

less clearly than the flute-songed nights
with their last owls whitefaced as moons
swooping low for the poisoned, dying mice.

The ghosts of wolves ring our hills.
Those birdcries, Comanche songs drifting
up from wartrails; the click of steel

in the night, prospectors or old soldiers
sharpening the edge of darkness to a keen
wind that blows all the stories away.

To the Marches of Wind, Summer

came with its quiet pipes of cloud,
smoke heavy on the vestry of mesas
clinging to the soft peaks of Sangre,
Sangre de Cristo, mountains of everyone's
boyhood

To see them is to wish again
for the swift legs and firm muscles
of youth, clear eyes or eyes clearing,
the thin clean air washing the hollows
of sockets and restoring sight, hearing.

Summer now has nearly passed to Fall.
We, those whom the mountains have held,
turn southward, moving down the pink adobe
washes of Santa Fe, past Algodones,
to the ancient villages of Tome and Los Lunas.

My car wheels sound to dimmed ears
a little like horse's hooves and levis
are not so far from armour and leather,
the clouds streaking flags all over the skies.

The Rock Collector

Old Doc Allison, a "doctor," in fun
or in grudging respect

       a hard drinker
with kindness and more knowledge
than we could cope with—Saver
of Small Boys, tortured cats,
dogs with tincans on their tails

—walking uncertainly down Main
Street, faultlessly dressed, his hat
brushed and slightly tilted, the cold
glare of the drugstore light caught
his red face, the deep lines . . .

He was once a famous geologist
the town said. We boys didn't care,
sensing in him the living boy, the
comrade by the way he talked to the night
(his many kindnesses, the shy looks)

When he died his wife threw out his
specimens, quartz, jagged crystals
more beautiful than diamonds, copper
ores, rare gemstones embedded in matrix,
caught sparkling in the sun of the alley-
way's dust

      We boys gathered them up
set them in an oval about his grave
on the Hill, watched the late sun
pick out the lights while the lamps
of the town darkened beneath us
and age caught us each up, glowing
in the new starlight, the hanging
dust . . . .

Luminarios

Centuries, Village within the Hills

Candleflames against time marred adobe,
her face luminous in nearly gone light,
dark skin of the Dark Madonna, cheap
print framed in tin and copper, the lights

catch on Indian cheekbones, Castillian hair,
soft lips open to the lines and quick lusts
that hours engrave upon a loved one's face.
Too heavy with history are these nights.

Temporary, easy, the hours slip by here. Dark
is a word she shuns in the blonde dreams
of ancestors who marched the aching land
hot with dreams of conquest and noble blood.

They did not attain to glory, only to adobe,
sheep bleating in the sun and a cool breeze
at evening to carry the sleep back to Spain.
Easy, easy, the centuries pass her by, lace

mantilla handed from daughter to daughter, this
one framed so closely by candlelight, the other
lights switched out at Christmas, she bends to
strike the fire and welcome Holy Travellers home.

—Christmas at Taos, New Mexico

The Arrival of My Mother

—New Mexico Territory, 1906

She got off, according to her diary,
dressed in a lovely beaded gown, fresh
from Washington with sixteen trunks of ballgowns,
chemises, blouses (4 Middie), shoes and assorted
lingerie. She was at that time about 25, old
for an unmarried woman. Her stiff mother was at
her side, she also wildly overdressed for New Mexico
sun and wind.

What must she have thought, seeing my uncle standing,
hat in hand in the dust of that lonely train house,
cracked yellow paint, faded letters of welcome
for passengers that rarely come?

The buckboard was waiting and they rode out into
the darkness of evening toward the tent, that half
built frame homestead house, wind dying as the sun
sank, birdcries stilled.

I see her now outshooting my father and me, laughing
at our pride and embarrassment. My sister, as good a
shot, waiting her turn. Or that picture of her
on horseback, in Eastern riding clothes beside the Pecos.
A picnic when I was small and how my father lifted me up
to her and she carefully walked the horse around rock
and sand.

I suppose she finally arrived in New Mexico
in the April of one year when my sister and I sat beside
a rented bed, each holding one of her hands and watched
her eyes grow childlike, unmasked as a *kachina*
entering the final *kiva* of this Dance. The graceful
the slim laughing woman of my childhood. The old mother
heavy with years slipped away and the woods of New
England dimmed as these dry hills ripened and caught
her last breath, drums, drums should have sounded
for the arrival of my mother.

12

A Lament for Old Cowboys

They hear voices, the old
whispers of the land, the blued
hoofbeats of their horses shatter
the stone arroyo's silence

    beside the mountain
    in soft mesquite dusk
    the flutter of eagle feathers
    shadows of lost ceremonials

Under concrete and asphalt
under these years of dust and longing
there are tracks: bobcats with high
yellow eyes, mountain lions, wolves
the smaller creatures fleeing before
them

    Peel the black road back and see
where the young cowpunchers passed
whooping, going to see the Elephant
riding the Tiger, hearing the Owl
hoot along trails we never found
the ending of

      the old voices of this land
sing in guitared darkness, cry and moan
as the wind rises, dust down an empty
road bright with moonlight, scudding clouds

        —The Goodnight-Loving Trail

To My Wife

There are beauties & beauties.
Yours are simple, rough
irregular

The boned lines of your face
stand, in certain lights, severe
almost harsh

You worry about seeming old

while I've watched your hands
sewing, seen the strong arcs
they make

        needle passing through
materials drawing firm together
thread lost in weave:

a wholeness, coming together
lost in itself from attention.
We are what we piece together

beauty after beauty the hand
your hand turns in the light, the tuck
is made

There are these beauties & then
there is you, lined fingers following
the silver needle, sewing light
into place

The Streets of San Miguel

What have I to bring them, in their
stillness?

       dark youths lounging
by the one public phone, old ladies
headed for Mass, the soft wind
against their black dresses.

       If I lived here all my life,
spoke Spanish as fluently as I dream I do,
if one of these lovely boys loved one
of my lovely girls & I was elected mayor,
still I'd be a broken Anglo poet
who has, I'm told, strange eyes,
stranger ways—

       who must turn
everything to words while they, so alive
need so few to speak their loves.

The dusty street, quiet in moonlight,
stretches out ahead. I take a strange walk,
going nowhere. I have nowhere to go.
The ancient houses ring a pathway
to high, windswept mesas.

Sketches for an Old Land, an Old People

Santa Catalina Crest, Overlooking Tucson

The rock cliffs are porous
whistle in the wind blowing
from the city far

        below it
        glitters, moves

   —as it touches these crags, the
field resolves, clears, dust rises
against a horizon where desert also moves
toward mountain

        Here the wind
        traces out my veins the
        great roar of mountain
        is underfoot, blood a
        solid pulse, reaching

toward sky, these pines
talk to sky, rock dissolves under me.

Old Women beside a Church

the blackshawled women of New Mexico
wait, wait outside their churches, in the
gusty winds, their black dresses

in frail silk & gauze they wait, widows
of Christ, faces stiffly furrowed

cracked to mud they watch, eyes centered
deep in the

        clanging bell

enter
burn candles for a soul, for
cold beds, flickering oil lights
the wind brushes adobe walls away
grain by grain

Coyotes Fighting

Turning, orange and black, dream
crimson

      teeth white with moonlight

the blood more an illusion than
a part of their own curiously fierce
laughter
      even the fight
a joke for bitches, showoffs, *coyotes*
on a ricepaper background, fragile
as the soft pads of their feet, circling.

—from a woodcut by George Vlahos

The New Mexican

From one of the draws, out of a mountain
across plains heavy with grass or dry
bleached and cracked by the sun

                                        he came,
rifle easy in his hand, a hunting dogtrot
in his heart, brain singing with the hunt,
the need for a kill

                          Old mountain men, born
and raised for the power of their hands & arms,
valuing themselves little past those physical
strengths, and what survival finally cost them
when the necessities, time, disappeared
with the game

Old men, sitting on porches or scratching out
gardens, their blue black brown green eyes
cutting out a trail that now only hawks
dare follow

                    Out of the North, come the snows,
falling on storebought windows. Old men get
laid in frozen earth, their big hands holding
scars like lilies the coming springs
may never bear again . . . .

back to back, Stud Poker & an open
pot. The play, intense, grew harder.
Clark, Bowers, McMorris & my dad, cool
professionals: "Poker's for men," my dad'd
say, paying out his debts with grocery money,
bringing his tales with flushed face to our
quiet home. Great stories from the tall
fierce combats he lived for

      while I, a comrade,
a spy posted by mother, sat by propping
my eyes open & pleasing father who thought
at last I'd shown a normal interest.

      Thick cigar smoke
& the sharp smell of whiskey, I remember
that, & the naked bulb, those men
flicking cards into the pot of light
slitted eyes watching their fall
as if it were their own:

      yet my father won
with a slipped ace & we got out quick
before the discards were counted. Walking
home, 4 a.m., my father singing & looking
back over his shoulder, the quiet street
behind him.

      —for Richard Russell

Lincoln County War

the high green. tall, brightspun
pines, dark earth rich with tales
of the War.

       Tunstall, McSween, Brewer,
Bonney

       —blued guns flaming out
from ambush or siege, hooves
breaking the mountain night, guns

legends of hate, still remembered
as a kind of pride long after
the flashing hands are buried:

       growing up, among those
       ghosts, their fierce needs
       for courage, stiffness

A heritage of murder. The Kid
his queer laugh, high, hysterical.

O'Folliard, Bowdre who rode beside
him

       buried there, with him.

Blazer's Mill where Dick Brewer,
the Kid and some others trapped
Buckshot Roberts, killed him

       Roberts shot Brewer, wounded
       two others though he
       couldn't lift his arms
       above his waist, so shot
       up was this tough old man

—a legacy fit for
New Mexico, for grim old gunmen,
pistoleros who survived, telling
no stories, their deeds following
them in whispers

        walking stiffly down a
        street, they were old men,
        but the people got out
        of their way, their
        straight eyes, shiny
        imaginary guns swinging
        at their sides:
                    the glint
        of blue, high pines &
        gunfire, an empty trail
        leading out before them.

Hill Man

First he and his wife lived here
with their Spanish daughter
& stunted Indian-Spanish
son-in-law.

Then she died and he, tall,
whip-hard, stood alone in the neat yard
his new clothes too big for him
choosing not to see suburbs surrounding him.

—Staring toward the high, pale mountains
of his manhood, where his wife and he
tended sheep in the blue air . . . .

Once he took my blonde baby
held her in his arms and said
"*Qué linda tú eres, Chica.*" Gently.
He drew the sign of the Cross
on her soft forehead, for witches,
he said, were everywhere, still watch
from the mountains and would curse
a beautiful child praised
and without protection.

A big Jack, cutting outwards toward blue,
little puffs of my bullets hurrying him.
Sage crushed underfoot, crisp & clean—

My father, a big Irishman, redfaced & watching,
he who could hit anything within range,
who brought a 150-lb. buck three miles
out of the high mountains when he was 57

—a man who counted misses as weaknesses,
   he whipped up his own rifle, stopped the Jack
   folding him in midair, glanced at me, stood
   silent

My father who never knew I shot pips from cards
candleflames out (his own eye) who would've
been shamed by a son who couldn't kill. Riding
beside him.

The Brujo of Santos: A Folktale

Alejandro, maker of leather,
stood only as tall as his ancient bench.

According to people's talk, he rode that
bench, astraddle, across the moon-veined sky

to rendezvous deep in granite, unknown hills,
there to dance where the old gods hid.

Alejandro, maker of leather, once named witch,
who one day found his huge wife impaled

upon his brother's larger member
and gouged his own eyes in grief.

Alejandro, who sits in his mother's village
bony back against a mudden wall.

His eyes are blind in this morning's sun.
I've seen it, he flies not at all.

Poem Beginning with a Line by Winfield Townley Scott

The pan-pipes child changed to a man somewhere

and left us, whether we would be left or not,
quickly, with hardly a wave of the hand
to let us know that he had come to a different
path, a turning, was gone his own way.

We looked up, and the path was empty, silent
ahead, stretching out a brown ribbon clear
to the horizon. Night was falling,
there were no pipes ahead, none behind.

And yet we keep to the trail he followed.

All of us the same, in heart, men who only
borrow the skins and pipes of gods and who must
lie them down at last, leaving a holy silence,
an uncleared road, a testimony to loneliness.

Winfield Townley Scott
1910-1968

The Horses

(two paintings by Hsu Pei-hung)

It's the way I conceive myself sometimes:
hammerheaded, bigfooted, but running loose
in black meadows.

                             Just at dusk,
the rice paper crashing beneath my hooves
every muscle a brushstroke, heavy with pigment, I,

                                alive with the race
                           of line, up, out.

ii

Or his five horses, standing in a field
looking over far gates or running hard & black
off shining paper.
                         All five are real enough
to ride, mine, a blaze on his forehead, slashes
the turf with his black hooves, neighs, and
thunders into my livingroom, shitting on the floor.
Damned horses that break a man's home up!

—short for Zebediah, late come
mountainman, part-time prospector
now grown stiff in the joints.
Unshaven but not bearded, bushy
eyebrows hanging over blue

At 83 my empty rifle moves smoothly
up to his shoulder, the hammer falls:
"A little stiff in the trigger, son,"
he says and looks away

                his half-wolf dog
moves moves with him, flank brushing
the old man's leg, big flat head down
he watches

         Once I made the mistake
of trying to touch him. He growled
deep in his chest. "Don't do that,
boy," Zeb said calmly. "He'll take your
hand off." And hobbled back to his
son's house, his lame old dog beside him.

Vision

We sat, you and I,
upon a bridge and watched
dry sand blow by.

Nothing in that.
Sand, and a view of change,
rough wind upon our skins.

To love the desert marks
one, leaves him both alone
and claims him, your hand

slips into mine the way
the sun glides down
to sudden night, the fierce

desert nights of owl
and swift snake. Moon
white as the wind dies

your face drives the night
the small clouds of evening
darken now about your hand.

The Drums Within Us All

Poem for the Mountain Gods

—Mescalero Apache Ceremonials

: with rhythmic interplay

& beyond the drums, migrant faces
vagrant, in motion

      behind
brush *wickiups* the fast drumbeats, high voices
rising to

      sweet smoke

hardwood lodgepoles slick
sweating in the mountain sun

      a dance for the Mountain Gods

for eagles, brought briefly
to earth while we sit waiting
watching

      teenage Apaches
      torment a snake (harmless)
      they laugh
      & I remember

      how Apaches long ago
      cut the rattles from diamondbacks
      released them near white settlements

the whole myth that is Apache

      (a handsome people
      a warrior people
      very straight with flint spark
      eyes full of warmth, direct

& now, toward evening, the dances begin:

devil dancers, *gan* dancers, clay moving in streaks
of sharp mountain lightning
towards the white clayed stomach
of the huge dancers
                            two groups, together
                            yet apart

                                holding a cross &
                                a sword, leaping figures
                                caught in showers of sparks
                                the great logs
                                snapping & burning

                        —caught in, before flames, a
                        mountain stillness the
                        drums & singers, singers

                        silencing all but
                        the blood

myth that is dance. With rhythmic
grace the women slowly
circle
a pounding center

—the leaping dancers
   flames

bright blankets
clutched about their breasts
the women
move around
mountain.

ii

: after silence

a time to breathe
before the drums begin again.

In the great teepee fragrant pine
& spruce hold to a cone
the pitted fire

young girls
in old buckskins once white
now yellowing listen

soft chants
start, drums

—a buffalo hide beaten outside
   by boys, tin drum

held between the singers
whose voices fill with joy

as in the teepee
the maidens circle, slowly
circle

            the standing flames

& night is an eagle
carrying dark hills away.

iii

: what it is to be here!

to feel mountain
as different from desert

knowing cold rocks, moist earth
I lie, trying not to sleep, listening

>   the drums building
>   wilder the dream
>   one dances to

the forever up! resents
any pause, any break in motion
which contained is nothing

>   like drunkenness
>   is a singing
>   between the ribs
>   —a defiance, a love

with darker pulses, breaking
into light
into showers of sparks
from broken logs
shattered by flames

the now distant Apache ceremonial
drums, & a clear singing goes up, showers
of sparks to light
a mountain night.

iv

: dreaming

dreamed, those dancing girls, leaping
men, a fantasia of blood
(which does not forget)
moon, already risen
climbs cool & white over the pines
& the drums go on
till dawn.

Talpa House

Last night drums from the plaza.
This morning, clear sunlight through the door,
water lies in two puddles from the hailstorm
early last evening. The children shout on their ways
to the ditch and high adventure in four inches of water.

The heavy *vigas* fan out, rays of the sungod's badge,
as chocolate adobe, the rich earth of my father's hills,
softens the morning light downstairs. One enters
a cedar and earth cave streaming with shadows,
pictures, and weavings, Navajo and Dorothy's.

In the bookcase are Bob's books, the fine lines
the graceful humorous words push open the house
until nothing is hidden here. Always an outsider
I walk the flagstone floors and feel less like a spirit
haunting things no man could ever own, but only hold
briefly, as a sunset touches light a dusty glass
or as the wind catches the top of an apple tree
and passes on to ruffle the fur of some jackrabbit.

I've had the feeling for days that deer were watching.
What they see in us, is for them to say. I wish
things were different. They could come out, with no
fear, but of course we understand and perform our tasks,
the children at their fabled dramas, Heloise humming,
I at these pages, typing black words on pages of sunlight.

—for Robert & Dorothy

Climbing in the Organ Mountains

—with Howard McCord & Turtle

Rocks underfoot slide, fall
down arroyos. Below, they rise,
sharp retorts, the distant firing
of guns, sporadic shirrr! of rattles

Ahead, the Caves: *Las Cuevas,*
ritual centers of the mountains,
drumbeaten to centuries of chants
—Indian magicmen dancing, singing

My small daughter Turtle Earthforce,
Ancient Mask of God loses her footing
almost falls. I catch her warm hand,
her happy voice, no fear, laughing

at rocks below, all the old ghosts
awakening, sleepy, full of pollen,
they stretch and yawn as we three
bear eaglefeathers up an ancient trail.

Late Afternoon at the Lawrence Ranch

—Taos, 1972

The sounds of calvary cross the hills.

Thunder in the mountains. Here the eye sweeps
vastly. Jemez to the west. Pine trees heavy
with the wind they support, sway with peace.

I am of these hills: their heavy bodies bear
and support me. Ghost voices in twilight.
The trees answer with their needled voices
my own quieted longings, my secret whispers.

Old gods touch, probe these machine-made clothes,
emptying the pockets, unbuttoning the shirt,
cleansing my skin with their quick winds.
Gently they force my eyes open, wide open . . .

History is a vision, a way of looking,
caught too often in the time peculiar to books.
The Spanish passed this way. Before them, Utes,
Dog Soldiers, Comanches, headed for Taos.

> *Mountain men once walked these hills,*
> *wolf eyes on brush and thicket.*

I sit here, son of this land, these valleys,
and history is the water I wash myself with,
watching centuries spill down these dry hillsides
explode into the valley, shouting like children.

40

Winter Song

> *But whistle it round*
> *the season can't wait*
> —Judson Crews

And we, walking through darkened woods,
Aware, if ever we are, of shadows
Hard and branched like the antlers
Of lost deer, St. Hubert's flaming
Cross, held between horns, Christ's
Eyes looking back across the years.

A hunter stopped on the needled trail,
His breath in clouds before him,
World slipping through the brush
Testing the wind, him

    for all the seasons
    a truce, a meeting
    gone past desire

    that they shall lie
    down together, lamb
    lion, deer

      we too
    softly loving in the
    grass hardening to winter,
    caught tight in the smaller
    winds of the valleys, rose
    dark as your eyes in love

We move in the sunlit woods, quiet
To the scent of musk, feet following
The Old Trail, aspens like prayer sticks
Blow across skies stiff with winter.

Colorado Poem

Prophet Rock, Colorado
—for Bob & Lee Byrd

Ringed round by snow
& ridged peaks

San Juan
Sangre de Cristo

The blood of Christ
dripping golden red
at sunset, sun

rise like a resurrection
it breaks, flows in colors
solid as the mosses & rocks

Here, in this valley
beauty gets caught small in the
dried turf of high desert plains

—Dutch Reformed Churches,
houses stiff as Grant Wood
or flat as Peter Hurd

washed colors you can touch
feel as textures close
to your bones.

But it all fades,
passes before the Stone
Hand pointing: the Way West.

Rock of the Prophet.

A fierce face & rich
robes of stone
The accusing finger that

in your dreams, suddenly
shifts, points at *you*
& you know for once

how far
is this West
you call your home.

ii

An eagle's nest
heavy with straw & shit.
Abandoned, broken.

Like man, Wolfe said,
eagles foul their nests
stuff their chicks

with the leavings
of the spinning world.

iii

    Cold air. Desert signs.
    Footprints in the late snows.

A memory of Utes, drifting
Sioux, Nez Perce
after the battle

      Chief Joseph
      Looking Glass
      Red Cloud

Old ghosts to stalk
a trail we try to walk
in our white skins we bear

longing Indian hearts.
Every American is an Indian!
That is their victory.

We who destroyed them
carry their medicine
dream their dreams

& from every mountain
we hear drum beats
celebrating

one final ceremony
drowning in our blood
the tears of their Trail

—lifting our hands, palms
up we see Hero Twins
Godfaces

with mountains for eyes
the desert quiet
for a heart.

Our dying locked magically
in theirs. These long trails.
Game steps in the silence of late snows.

Joy Song

> *Wem willst du klagen, Herz?*
> —Rilke

Out of this farcome light, the blue
flat mesa crisp — stern: moon
stars, land rushing in, in

My son & I walk the ditchbank
in silence, warmed to the coldwind
by each other's nearness

An Irish warrior-son he
carries his stiff bamboo spear
easily, the hills of distant loves lie
beyond the winter's light:

                a windless flight
of crying birds streaks the air
between our bodies

> *To whom, heart, would you complain?*

A waving sadness, grasping me
like a small hand, the pain
—that of being no longer alone—
the warm smell of piñoned fireplace smoke
& hearths to rest all the spears upon

Strata Laid on in Rocks

To what do old men portend?
In omens of tired eyes,
mysteries. Blue mountains.

Simple daily visions (In this
land, history crowds the shoulders
& rock measures a man's changes.)

Sleep. Sleep, old men. Close
your eyes, shuttering the masked
dancers reflected, waiting there.

To what do old men portend?
Out of parchment skins, thin
almost transparent, their spirits

look restlessly out, once more
before silence. Dreams go troubled,
are difficult to separate: was it

now, or yesterday she came
to me? My love, my love—
& what was her name, when

did she live, with whom? Omens
omens that we come to, carving these
strange charms shallowly into rock.

The dance drums have begun: out
of a central *kiva*, long forgotten
ceremonials proceed. Fires are

lighted, and strange gods sit
on rooftops, calling out our secret names
while dancing feet shatter the earth.

Cuentos para hoy

Homestead Revisited

—for Drum & Diana

In Guadalupe Canyon, named for Her,
Dark Madonna of everybody's America,
swift Lady of streams and dry mesas

(my godfather, don Virginio Casaus,
his lost rancho named Guadalupe, Lupe,
the name of a girl I never touched
but loved as a passing shadow of flame
peripheral to the boundaries of my hopes)

Thick sycamores with trunks of other
trees twenty feet up in the branches,
relics of a flood that swept the canyon
two years ago. More birds than I have seen
since boyhood days filled with fluttering wings.

My friend, Drum, rising to ride his horse
moving across the dust and stone in the old dance
of man and mount and land, dissolving blue
and brown shape in the mirage of heat and mountain.

Later, trying to ride myself on a horse
called Zopilote, turkey buzzard, and well-named,
who sensing my lack of confidence, my unease
in the once familiar saddle, tries to run
me through a thicket, tries literally to kill me
and a flash of memory hits

                        at *that* moment
of Apache, his mean tricks. Roberto, *mayor domo*
of a nearby Mexican rancho says, drinking tequila,
"*Caballos son malos.* You can't trust horses, my friend.
Did you know that they can kick in almost any direction
and will, for no cause a man can determine?" *Malo.* Beautiful.
Running free, forms as swift and graceful as She, Guadalupe,
sorrells and pintos and appaloosas, morgans and men
all caught to the dangerous ritual of men and cattle and horses.

At night, the cries of boyhood dreams coming from
the hills. Doves, coyotes, owls all on their own trails,
knowing the limits of their perceptions as I know my mind:
the wholeness of souls that have lived, worked and ridden
these dark hills where the moon only lightens spots
on the old earth, leaving shadows to hold mysteries,
hunting snakes.

            As I blow out the lantern, the years
spin back to a childhood I had tried not to remember,
the loneliness and uncertainty, the watchfulness of hills
and rocks, my boyish knowledge that they and I were one,
formed in the same way, and as old, riding the dark trails
of the Madonna, on Her ranch, in Her radiant canyons of moon.

WOLF TRIPTYCH

The Morning of the Wolf

The first time I saw him, he rose
out of the grass of a hill, his eyes
straight into mine, big head low

He moved toward me, ignoring the man
who stood beside me with the gun, his eyes
straight into mine. I was thirteen,
taught to hate and fear wolves. He, a *lobo*,
a Mexican wolf from below the border.
His eyes. I keep coming back to that.
The way they bore the center of me.

The gun began firing wildly, bullets
splashing dust around the wolf but he
hardly moved, his eyes never left mine
until I broke the contact and saw the man
his hands shaking, spraying the .22 bullets,
caught completely in buck fever, the wolf
almost laughing, eased off through the grass
his tail a contemptuous banner

—his every movement sure of the morning, me,
the long years I would remember his yellow eyes
that big head looking at me

                I recall the smell of sage
and creosote, the fear of that man, courage
of the wolf. Held in my brain, he never
went away at all. His footsteps sound outside
my city window. His cry rises and falls
on the dawn wind.

The Day of the Wolf

The other ranchers came this morning,
early; in the crisp blue air of Fall
they stood stiffly—each holding his reins
his restless horse, took coffee, nodding
a "thank-you-mam," his rifle hanging
beside him in a scratched leather
scabbard

          —the wolf was back, three calves
slaughtered yesterday, their white faces flat
on the ground, big eyes splattered with dirt

: Wolf, running free past the traps in search
of fresh meat. he couldn't be fooled by bait.

That evening we got him just the same,
shot him down when he came to smell
the bitch coyote we'd staked out,
got him, horses in a circle he
couldn't cross, but he fought well,
stood his ground, slugs slapping
him down, him getting up, snarling
showing his teeth until he died.

The horses wouldn't carry his hide
back and we left it there, bloody in the
dusk, his skinny body white as a child's
in the waving tall grass.

The Night of the Wolf

A day, an hour, and it's gone, those years
when fences were rare, game everywhere: New
Mexico

        His wolf face looking at me
that hillside in a childhood sun
the fear and fascination of his eyes how
I saw them then, changing, the flecked
yellows, silvered fur, long blunt muzzle
his quick feet and confidence

They killed him, as he killed,
but they didn't eat him.
He would have eaten them.

He's back. I saw him last night.
He came to talk to me I think,
to tell me of the ruin of this land
(he wouldn't know how sick I am with it)
He didn't say anything of course,
what do wolves say?
He only looked at me, his eyes
full of concern and then he trotted off.

The game's gone and, I guess, we're going
to go with it. Predators need game, they
can't live without it. That wolf and I
are brothers, or why would he have come,
why warn me unless he thought I could do
something about it. I can't, I guess he
saw that, us both remembering that childish
hillside with its sun, him running so free,
rabbits popping up everywhere like furry flowers.

Yellow Green

are the colors of this land, if you add
brown, and blue for the sky, black
for the nights.
                I was opening or shutting
a barbed wire gate, walked around the car
to get in and saw his eyes, round, dark
watching me
              For a second I thought
he was a gopher snake, harmless . . . I'd raised
one for a year, became as much a friend
as a snake will permit, liked him deeply
and hated to turn him loose, to live
where he must, I where I must . . . .

Then he raised his viper's head and my eyes
traveled along his yellowish green smoothness
to where the rattles stood erect, quivering.

I could not hear them, but that is another
story coming out of the crash of gunfire
that surrounded my young manhood. For a second
I felt tightness, I knew him, Old Enemy
respected by the Indians and my father as wise,
fierce, uncompromising
              I knew our brotherhood.
I stretched out my hand. He didn't coil
nor did he relax and I squatted down just out
of striking distance. We talked. I tried
to explain how he must move from the road,
I would not hurt him. He seemed to understand,
the quiver of his rattles lessened, his head
lowered but he was uncertain, afraid, uneasy
of turning his back to me, a man.

I couldn't blame him. I too trust snakes more
than most men, believe them in their quick honesty.

Finally I threw some small clods near his head
so that he could see I was capable of hurting him
but chose not to . . . a logic wild creatures understand.

He crawled away, his beautiful body vivid in afternoon
sun, rattles still and my hand unconsciously reached
farther out to him.
               I, wishing I could follow and join
with his warm world of hunting and loving, tie myself
into a ball with him and his sisters and brothers, sleep
the long winter through, dreaming of rabbits and mice,
the sweet rites of spring

A rancher killed a snake the next morning.
He said it looked a lot like my friend.

The colors of this land are blood & bone.

The Arroyo

He walked there with his buddy,
both carrying .22's, hunting rabbits
for supper—down Yeso Creek, thin
slick stream running down
the center of the eroded arroyo.

He was walking close to the bank
when out of the brush a heavy stick
fell toward him, no rattle, just
struck. He leaped, dropping his
rifle and yelled—the giant diamond
back just missing him

        He picked himself up,
looked around. Snakes uncoiling
from their winter hibernation
slid across the sand and all around
him the whirring rattles began

Angry, hungry, the snakes probed,
hard flat heads back, cocked,
their rattles thundering in the draw,
the sand slid and grated under
his boots. He stood perfectly still.

Crack! The head of the nearest
snake dissolved and its body thrashed
almost touching him

    "Don't move. Everything will
be . . . Crack! . . . all right. Now just
you . . . Crack! . . . stand there, *bueno*?"

The barrel of the singleshot .22
was hot when his friend finished.
Later the two of them counted 11 snake
bodies, 5 or 6 that got away.

              —for my father

The Day of the Rabbit

Jackrabbbit: a shy, swift creature
with round, shiny eyes, fur
that ruffles in the wind

One Sunday, they rounded us kids up,
promising a picnic and loaded us into pickups.
Chattering, we rode through the dust, screaming
with joy and the bumps, any high fly through the air.

At the ranch all was nearly ready:
a huge beef turned and smoked on the spit,
pickles in barrels, beans in great clay pots,
red chilis crumpled into jagged flakes
and dropped into the bubbling brown sauce.
Dutch Oven biscuits, hot & steaming
being sampled by the cook.

The pickhandles were piled just beyond.
Each of us was given one, the details explained
by the potbellied rancher: we were to form
a huge circle, about two feet apart,
the men would join us, then we would close.

Later, moving slowly through the grass,
we scared up several rattlesnakes, various
small rats, a bird or two. The dust closed
on a tight pen in the center and there they
were. Over a hundred rabbits, cottontails
and big Jacks milling, trying to break free.

Then the rancher took a pickhandle from one
of the boys and, laughing softly, walked to
the pen and hit one of the rabbits, breaking
its back. The rabbit screamed high & shrill,
went on screaming, he hit another & another,
soon all the boys were in there, hitting, blood
all over them, the big eyes of the rabbits
shining out of the dust, their screams cutting
the air, boys shouting & the older men sat
back, watching, smoked their brownpaper Durhams
& smiled, thinking of the rich feed to come.

—Cambray, New Mexico, 1936

The Day of the Crow

The small sharpnesses of a boy's life.
My father whistling crisp and clear
as out of the Southwest's sunshine
Karl came winging, cawing out his needs.

Raw beef, bloody still from the knife,
chunks of bologna, cheese, civilized
bird of carrion, he perched lightly
upon my hand, flexing his hard talons

—the time he streaked silently down
to pounce upon my mother's Easter hat
rip the feather, tear the felt, screeching
out his rage and triumph over her tears.

"How would you feel," my sister said to her,
"if a crow wore a human skin before you?"
And mother listened for that was the way
she was and Easter came just the same.

Karl, his eye cocked, watched us eat
what he would never touch, we laughing
at his cleverness, his tricks and thefts.
Pens, knives flew glittering with his cries

as my own world grew crowded with the long days
of summer and coyotes, eagles my father found
and we returned later, grown, healthy, to the land
they owned and we only shared, the sleek brush

of Karl's black wings against my face stayed,
though he flew, he flew in black crowds of crow,
mated I think and slashed the clear light
back to my waiting hand. Until once

the crows flew by, unswerving, headed away
and out. My father found them later, circling
on the ground in their funeral dance, cawing
softly for the shotgunned figure that we buried
observing our rites, not theirs, on a cool evening
when sharp stars cut holes in a summer's night.

Bridge Over the Pecos

There was this story about a railroad bridge.
Eleven men died, fell into the wet concrete pillars,
were left there, stone men holding up the ties
spikes, the shining rails.

                       Others say white men
killed them. They were black, story goes, one
for each pillar, for luck, for the blood
that binds stone and locks it into place.

Later, a switching engine fell when the roadbed
shifted, it tumbled steaming, its bright wheels
whirling suns, fell its heavy black arc
into quicksand

                 Crew, engine and all sank beneath
the greysilver sands and are down there yet, dead
hand near the throttle.

                   Sun, rising over the Pecos, wind
wild in the cedar brakes, rabbits catching the scent
of foxes on their twitching noses, river run muddy
clouding the old stories, blurring the faces . . . .
How many deaths it takes to move a people across
a land
       Bridge, dead black marching pillars.
The bronze sun, Indian songs beside, quiet river.

                       —for my father
                        who knew the River
                        better than I

How to Bridle a Horse

—for Drummond Hadley
& his horse

Tough hammerheaded range horse, Turk,
riderwise, used to mornings, evenings—
now he stands by the corral, tosses
his head just enough to keep Drum
from getting the bit in his soft mouth.
Snorts, backs slightly, dance beginning.

Drum moves closer, talking, whispering,
bridle in one hand, fingers in the mane,
Turk, he shakes his head, Drum does too,
goes for a soft light rope, loosely knotting it,
works it around the hindfeet, Turk,
standing almost still, nostrils narrowing.

He waits—around the neck, the forelegs,
hold the head down! bridle slips up
and Turk's head rises arrogantly, taking
slack up, he knows it's just a matter of time,
"Turk," Drum says softly, the rope woven about
the strong neck, "Turk, Big Horse," words gently

enmeshing the wild eyes, his head up, up
knowing the web is winding about him, can't
move much now without breaking a leg,
his long neck straining, eyes looking
more trapped now, bridle sliding close,
in!
      Turk, not the least cowed, plays
the game to its end as Drum slumps,
exhausted, explaining it all . . . .

The Day of the Dog

He'd been appointed Town Marshall.
We boys, expecting Wyatt Earp, got him.
Almost fifty, fat with a red sweating face
& drunkard's eyes, he wore a dirty shirt
old trousers and shoes with no socks.

My uncle said his wife was a nice woman,
they gave him the job to keep him out of trouble.
There wasn't much in the Village, a few punchers
fighting on Saturday night, once in awhile a drunk
to jail. Morgan handled them real well. "He knows
the way," one man said laughing.

One day the Town Council told him to run
the strays dogs out of town because of rabies.
Since the old man could hardly walk, much
less run, they asked us to catch the dogs.
bring them to a pen and then, they said,
he'd take a pickup load off and come back
for the rest. A friend of mine asked, "How
come there's no cage? Them dogs will jump right
out, you know they will." But we didn't listen.

By four in the afternoon, we had 20 or 30 dogs,
males and bitches in the pen. Old Morgan drove
up, got out. We could see he was drunk, his
hand shook when he took out the slim .38 and
started firing blindly into the massed dogs.
Some of the kids yelled for him to stop
but he just reloaded and kept shooting, bullets
screaming off through the streets, men diving
for cover and the dogs howled, their blood running
in little rivers over the hard clay, him weaving
as he aimed the pistol, his star glinting in
the sun, the noise of each shot like a crashing
blow. Solemn, drunk, he did his duty and no one
dared stop him until the dogs were all lying there
dead or dying. Then the mayor strode up, took the gun
and led him back to his wife, who cried all
the time he told her how he'd fixed those
dogs, hadn't he, honey?

The Near Miss

The growing motor noise,
over mine, my own preoccupation,
the sense of being *correct*,
in phase, catching out of the corner
of my eye, the bluegrey motion,
the skidding tires, my own actions
so slow, almost dreaming, turning
the wheel

        and missing.
Yes, by *that* much the car loaded
with kids who waved, through
the fear that blanked their faces.

39 years old I thought suddenly.
I'm shaking, I said. Shaking.
To them, a dangerous game,
to me, survival. And was ashamed.

The broken back, the 3 concussions,
the shattered ankle, all the illnesses
the dislocated shoulder on that football
field, the slow pain, sense of people's
faces so glad it wasn't them. My own
shadow falling across the gutshot boy,
lying there, his face grey as the paint
below him. So much pain to be walked
through, carried by, moved away from.

Now, in a dusty Indian village with only
one real street, which I've driven a hundred
times, now to have it all come back,
driving along, my nervous hands
pretending I'm in control, and this
is a real street and not a whirlpool
at all

The Name-Giver

Driving through the Sacramento Mountains
three in the morning of a spring day.
Mountains of the Holy Sacraments, slender
pines whipping by in late starlight.

I had been driving since ten that morning.
Now, fighting sleep, unable to stop
because of the twisting narrow road
I listened to my Turtle daughter beside me
telling me her kind of jokes, her histories
of fabled animals—Keeping Daddy Awake
was what she later called it all.

I glanced out the window and running beside
the car in the crisp light was a naked man
with the head and eyes of a wolf. I saw his
firm trunk, the light fur over his chest
and stomach, the heavy bush and long penis
that swung between his thighs as he ran.

He was grinning and looking at me.
I thought of mentioning it to Turtle but
what if she didn't see him, I thought, how
would she handle that? Me seeing someone she
didn't. For a moment, I tried to pretend
he wasn't there, glanced back and sure enough
he was keeping up, effortlessly, looking at me
and smiling with his fine white teeth.

Something passed between us, I can't say what,
some look from our eyes, and just as the thought
began to enter my head that, wolf face or not,
he looked a lot like a younger me, he waved his
hand in salute and raced off into the darkness
of the pine trees.

                    My mind clear, I found a spot
soon and parked but couldn't sleep, sensing his form
moving through the brush, watching and guarding us.

An Indian would have said I had my name when I
awoke the sun and faint circle of the moon
were paintings on an old hide, carefully tanned
and held by chiefs against whatever darkness
of memory or charm might come to the tribe, the
children singing, Heloise driving now,
counting the miles to our house, its solid doors.

In Sere & Twisted Trees

—El Rito, New Mexico

Walking the small trails of stonecropped hills,
my son and I read with the grains of our skins
the old language, its tongues of night and day,
toned winds and the watching trees and skies.

How it all grows easy and secure when one realizes
everything is alive in the summer's sun, listening
watching. I speak to my brothers. I tell them
we are coming, meaning no harm. Wait. My son, 10,
is a fisherman, and he hopes to catch trout.
I tell them this, promise he will eat what he catches.
I will see to this.

A prayer for the trout.
A prayer for my son, whom I love more than ever
watching his graceful figure dance to the rod
and fly he made. I needn't have bothered the trout.
He was wiser than my son. We walk back, Kevin,
still excited, apparently not caring about the lack
of fish, full of the adventure of the day.

He no longer holds my hand now, and I understand.
His embraces are quick, embarrassed, his eyes
shifting warily away towards the hills. It won't
be long, as this canyon's time is measured,
before he leaves me. Pray for me, Trout.
Pray for me, Mountain Stream.

A Way Through the Mountains

Beyond the lava rock, the yucca
with its stiff blooms. Within
a hollow cut for the rising sun.
In the darkness, when he is not there
a small man sings His songs and watches
the small gestures of stars and planets.

I walk in beauty,
surrounded by beauty.
Every animal is my equal.
All that lives, my brother.

The small man kneels, tall and high
the rock rises from him, eagles cry
the great bears grunt about him.
At dawn he arises and Sunrays cut
A Way Through the Mountains for him
who sings the Sun home again.

O sing, sing to the home
in the clouds, where gods
walk within the skins of men
and Night's Daughter holds
a dark jeweled cup over
the world, moon sliding through
the sky's black waters

His song is of many things, his thoughts
of many more. Slowly he walks the Yellow
Path and the stones and spines are soft
to his bare feet. The eagles cry about him.
Bear-gods with eyes of sunlight walk with him.

In beauty happily I walk.
With beauty before me I walk.
With beauty behind me I walk.
With beauty above me I walk.

May there be happiness.
May there be success.
May there be good health.
May there be good feeling.

It is finished in beauty.

—from Pueblo & Navajo chants